Getting To Know...

Nature's Children

PRONGHORNS

Elma Schemenauer

PUBLISHER	Joseph R. DeVarennes
PUBLICATION DIRECTOR	Kenneth H. Pearson
MANAGING EDITOR	Valerie Wyatt
SERIES ADVISOR	Merebeth Switzer
SERIES CONSULTANT	Michael Singleton
CONSULTANTS	Ross James
	Kay McKeever
	Dr. Audrey N. Tomera
ADVISORS	Roger Aubin
	Robert Furlonger
	Gaston Lavoie
EDITORIAL SUPERVISOR	Jocelyn Smyth
PRODUCTION MANAGER	Ernest Homewood
PRODUCTION ASSISTANTS	Penelope Moir
	Brock Piper

EDITORS

Katherine Farris	Anne Minguet-Patocka
Sandra Gulland	Sarah Reid
Cristel Kleitsch	Cathy Ripley
Elizabeth MacLeod	Eleanor Tourtel
Pamela Martin	Karin Velcheff

PHOTO EDITORS	Bill Ivy
	Don Markle
DESIGN	Annette Tatchell
CARTOGRAPHER	Jane Davie
PUBLICATION ADMINISTRATION	Kathy Kishimoto
	Monique Lemonnier

ARTISTS

Marianne Collins	Greg Ruhl
Pat Ivy	Mary Theberge

This series is approved and recommended by the Federation of Ontario Naturalists.

OK

Canadian Cataloguing in Publication Data

Schemenauer, Elma.
  Pronghorns

(Getting to know—nature's children)
Includes index.
ISBN 0-7172-1933-X

1. Pronghorn antelope—Juvenile literature.
I. Title.   II. Series.

QL737.U52S33 1985   j599.73'58   C85-098731-8

Have you ever wondered . . .

when young pronghorns start to run?   page 6

if you could outrun a baby pronghorn?   page 6

if the pronghorn has any relatives?   page 9

where pronghorns like to live?   page 10

why you don't often see pronghorns in zoos?   page 10

how fast pronghorns can run?   page 12

what makes the pronghorn such a good runner?   page 15

who can run faster, a male pronghorn or a female?   page 16

why it's hard to see a pronghorn from far away?   page 19

why a pronghorn may look very messy in the spring?   page 20

where the pronghorn gets its name?   page 23

if female pronghorns have horns?   page 23

if it would be easy to sneak up on a pronghorn?   page 24

why pronghorns might follow a coyote around?   page 27

what pronghorns like to eat?   page 28

if pronghorns will jump over fences?   page 31

whether pronghorns do much traveling?   page 31

how male pronghorns attract mates?   page 32

where a mother pronghorn goes to have her babies?   page 35

what a newborn pronghorn looks like?   page 36

how a mother pronghorn protects her babies?   page 39

if pronghorn kids like to play?   page 40

how pronghorns warn each other of danger?   page 44

how long pronghorns may live?   page 46

"Home, home on the range
  Where the deer and the antelope play . . ."

Have you visited the western plains, North America's "blue sky country"? If so, you may have seen a shy, fleet-footed pronghorn, or antelope as the song calls it, bounding across the wide open spaces.

The Blackfoot Indians of the western plains told this story about the pronghorn: Long ago the Old Man (God) was in the mountains. He took some earth and made a pronghorn. Then he let it loose to see how it would run.

The pronghorn bounded up a steep slope. But there were many rocks in the mountains. The poor pronghorn ran so fast that it fell and hurt itself on the rocks.

The Old Man saw that the mountains were not the right place for the pronghorn. So he took it down to the plains. There he let it loose again. Again the pronghorn ran like the wind. But this time it ran gracefully. It looked so happy streaking across the windswept prairie that the Old Man knew he had found just the right spot for it!

Playful Pronghorns

Even baby pronghorns are good runners. By their second day of life, pronghorns have already taught themselves to run. They are still a bit shaky on their feet, though. Probably if you ran after one, you could still catch it.

The next day, however, you wouldn't have a chance of catching it. The baby pronghorn would already be running too fast for you. And by its seventh day, it would run faster than most dogs and horses!

No wonder young pronghorns love running games. They prance around in circles. They chase each other as if playing tag. They even run group races. Several youngsters will speed away from their mothers, swing around in a big circle and then race back to their waiting mothers.

Mother pronghorns often lie down to rest. Sometimes, just for fun, the baby pronghorns jump from the back of one resting mother to another. How do you think the mothers like such bouncing babies?

Opposite page:

A bundle of energy!

A Small Family

Like deer, goats and cattle, pronghorns eat plants. And, like these animals, they also have split hoofs. But although you might think a pronghorn looks somewhat like a small deer, it is not closely related to deer. For that matter, it is not closely related to goats or cattle either.

In fact, pronghorns have no close relatives anywhere in the world. They belong to a family all their own.

Early explorers thought pronghorns were antelopes, and some people still call them by that name. Other people call them pronghorn antelopes. Pronghorns, however, are not related to the antelopes of Africa and Asia, and the correct name for them is really pronghorn.

Can you guess how this elegant animal got its name?

Home on the Range

Pronghorns are found only on the plains of the North American west and in central Mexico. In Canada, they live on the sagebrush-dotted prairies of southern Alberta and Saskatchewan. In the United States, most pronghorns live on the range lands of Wyoming and Montana. Occasionally some can be found roaming the ranges from Iowa west to the mountains along the Pacific Coast.

When explorers first came to North America, there were huge herds of pronghorn all over the western plains. Today, however, it is not so easy to see a pronghorn, because they live only in the most deserted parts of the great plains, far from fences, buildings and people. Since pronghorns are nervous creatures they do not live long when kept as zoo animals or pets. They seem to need the freedom of the open range.

The shaded area of this map shows where pronghorns live.

Prairie Speedsters

Pronghorns love to run. They even like racing with moving objects.

People who drive cars through pronghorn country are often surprised when a group of pronghorns suddenly appears from behind a low hill and starts running beside the car. Faster and faster the animals bound along, trying to stay ahead of the car.

All at once the animals put on a burst of speed. Then they cut across the road *in front of* the car!

Once the pronghorns have crossed the road, they seem to feel the race is over. They stop and stare at the car and driver, looking pleased with themselves.

Pronghorns have been clocked at speeds as fast as 95 kilometres (60 miles) per hour. Some people believe pronghorns are one of the fastest large mammals in the world—second only to the cheetah.

The pronghorn is the fastest running animal in North America.

Born to Run

A close look at a grown-up pronghorn shows that it is built to run. The pronghorn has very large hoofs for the size of its body. These hoofs have firm, but bouncy, pads underneath that help to keep the animal's feet from getting sore as it pounds across the plains. The pronghorn also has strong, well-developed muscles in its slim legs.

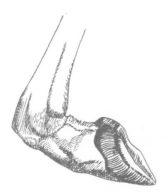

Pronghorn hoof

Surprisingly, the pronghorn's body is rather chunky. A full-grown pronghorn stands about one metre (3 feet) high at the shoulder. It weighs about 45 kilograms (100 pounds).

You might not think such a chunky body would be good for running fast, but it is. Inside its wide chest, the pronghorn has a super-sized windpipe, large lungs and huge heart. The pronghorn's heart, for instance, is twice as big as a sheep's heart, yet the two animals weigh about the same.

Pronghorns often seem to run for the sheer fun of it.

Keeping Up The Pace

Have you ever run hard and then had to stop because you were out of breath and your muscles hurt too much to keep going? It takes a long time for this to happen to a pronghorn. That is because its body is built to take in lots of oxygen and to quickly carry away the wastes (such as lactic acid) that make the muscles ache. Such a well-equipped body allows this prairie speedster to run fast over long distances. The pronghorn's endurance makes it a long-distance champ!

Female pronghorns, called does, can run faster than males, called bucks. A playful doe may tease a buck by getting him to run after her. Often she leads him on a long and merry chase.

Pronghorns believe in "safety in numbers." Gathering together is one way they have of defending themselves from their enemies.

A Coat That Blends In

The pronghorn's coat is a gray, tan or reddish brown color, just like the sun-baked prairie earth. Its cheeks, throat, belly and rump are white. Smart-looking black markings trim its face and throat.

This "blend-in" color scheme makes the pronghorn hard to see from far away. When standing still, it almost seems to disappear among the brownish shrubs and grass of the dry plains. This camouflage helps protect it from predators.

All Weather Coats

The pronghorn's coarse, hairy coat also helps keep it comfortable in all kinds of weather. This coat is actually two coats in one. Long guard hairs keep out rain and snow, while short inner fur helps keep out the cold in winter.

When the hot sun bakes the prairie, the pronghorn uses special muscles to make its guard hairs stand up straight. This helps to let the cool breezes through.

When cold winds howl across the prairie, the pronghorn flattens its guard hairs. They overlap to form a cozy "blanket."

Just as you probably have different coats for winter and summer, so does the pronghorn. In late fall, it grows a thick, warm winter coat. It sheds this coat in spring. A shedding pronghorn can look very messy with thick folds of old hair hanging from its sides.

A molting pronghorn is a messy-looking pronghorn.

Special Headgear

The pronghorn gets its name from its branched, or pronged, horns. The headgear of the pronghorn is different from that of any other animal in the world.

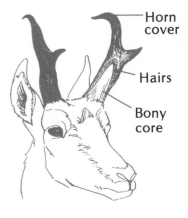

Cutaway of pronghorn's horn

Horn cover

Hairs

Bony core

Deer, elk and moose grow antlers. Antlers are solid bony growths. They are branched, and the animals shed them every year. Pronghorns, on the other hand, do not grow antlers. They grow true horns like the horns of cattle, sheep and goats. These are hard, hollow covers over bony cores. They are not *solid* bony growths like antlers.

Every fall the pronghorns shed their hollow horn covers. The bony cores remain and are covered with special hairs. These hairs are the beginnings of new horn covers that will take seven to eight months to reach their full growth. Pronghorns are the only animals in the world that shed their horn covers every year.

The horns of the males can be quite large. They often grow to be 25 centimetres (10 inches) long or even longer. Female pronghorns usually have much smaller horns or, sometimes, none at all.

Opposite page:

Pronghorn buck.

23

All The Better To See You With

Pronghorns have huge, jet black eyes and can see very, very well. Their eyes are even larger than those of a horse, which is a much bigger animal.

A man was once looking for pronghorns with a strong pair of field glasses. He spied a buck on a ridge almost two kilometres (one mile) away. To his surprise, the man saw that the buck was staring right back at him!

The pronghorn could see just as well as the man with the field glasses—probably better. Many people believe a pronghorn can see about eight times farther than a human can. This sharp eyesight is important for an animal that lives on the open prairie. It needs to be able to see predators from far off. Because of its good eyesight, it is very difficult to sneak up on a pronghorn.

Believe it or not, the large eyes of a pronghorn can detect movement over six kilometres (4 miles) away.

The Watchful Eye

Pronghorns are very inquisitive and seem to enjoy observing the behavior of other animals. Sometimes they trail along behind a coyote simply to watch it hunt mice and other small animals. (The coyote is probably not very pleased to have an audience along.)

Road builders also tell stories about curious pronghorns. They have seen pronghorns stand on a ridge for hours, watching the men and their machines at work. At any sign of danger, however, these shy, nervous animals turn and speed away.

Pronghorns' curiosity is easily aroused, but they do their watching from a safe distance.

Buttercups for Breakfast

Pronghorns are dainty, careful eaters. They nibble a few leaves and flowers here . . . some twigs there . . . a bit of bark somewhere else. Their favorite summer foods are clover, buttercups, wild onions and alfalfa. In spring, they find fresh grass shoots especially tasty. In winter, they paw through snow to find plants and shrubs, such as sagebrush.

Pronghorns do little harm to the prairie landscape as they eat. They step carefully and do not trample plants they are not eating. This means they leave few signs behind to show where they have been feeding.

Like a deer or cow, the pronghorn is a cud chewer. As it eats it collects unchewed food in a special part of its stomach. Later, it lies down to rest. That's when it brings its food, or cud, back up to its mouth for chewing.

The pronghorn may feed at any time of the day, but it is most active during the early morning and late afternoon.

933201

Finding Food in Winter

If there is enough food, pronghorns may spend months in an area only five to six and a half kilometres (3-4 miles) across. They are not great travelers. This may be partly due to the fact that roads, fences and train tracks now divide up much of their home range. Since pronghorns will not jump over even low fences, it is often difficult for them to travel far.

When winter arrives, however, pronghorns head for sheltered valleys. Here it takes longer for snow to cover the ground, so food is easier to find. As winter progresses, and the snow begins to deepen in the valley, pronghorns head for steep, windswept hillsides where the snow tends to be blown away. They look for the places with the most food and the least snow. Having to paw for their food as they struggle through deep snow would take up a lot of energy that would otherwise keep them warm.

Overleaf:

The pronghorn is a good swimmer and will not hesitate to cross a river.

Mating Dance

In late summer, pronghorn bucks begin to behave oddly. With their eyes protruding, they lower their heads and wave them from side to side. Then they quickly jump to the left and the right. As they do this, they ruffle their rump fur in wave-like motions. What is going on?

It is mating time and this is the bucks' way of attracting females.

A pronghorn buck usually gathers a harem of several does. Until mating season is over, he will chase away any other buck that tries to approach them.

Pronghorn buck trying to impress a group of does.

32

Springtime Babies

By spring, the pronghorn doe is ready to give birth.

Unlike many animal mothers, she does not make a den or a nursery nest. Instead, when she is about to give birth she looks for a secluded place away from the herd. Often she chooses a spot that has lots of tall plants around it so that she and her babies will not be seen. There she usually has twins, although one or three babies are not uncommon.

Does seek privacy when they are about to give birth.

Big Eyes

A baby pronghorn, or kid, seems to be all eyes, ears and legs. Its eyes and ears look too big for its narrow face. Its "toothpick" legs seem too long for its bony little body.

You may be surprised to learn that a newborn pronghorn weighs a little less than a newborn human baby. The average baby pronghorn weighs about two kilograms (4.5 pounds). Weights vary, however. Some pronghorn kids weigh as little as one kilogram (2.2 pounds)

As soon as the kids are born, the mother licks them all over to clean them. This also helps take away any of her scent that may linger on them. Since very young kids have almost no scent themselves, predators, such as coyotes, bobcats, golden eagles or foxes, will be unable to sniff them out.

Cute kid!

Lying Low

For the first week or so of its life, a pronghorn kid spends most of its time alone in its own special hiding place, called a cache. It lies flat on the ground, hidden by tall weeds and bushes.

The pronghorn mother does not stay right with her babies, because her scent might draw predators to them. Instead, she finds herself a spot a short distance away, usually about 400 metres (440 yards). From there she keeps a close watch on her babies' hiding places.

At this age the kids live on their mother's milk, and she visits them several times a day so they can nurse. However, before she goes to feed them, she looks all around to make sure there is no danger.

Sometimes a coyote or other predator comes near a kid's cache. If the predator gets too close, the mother tries to lead it away. If this does not work, she turns and fights. She kicks hard with her sharp hoofs. Usually a determined mother pronghorn can drive away a hungry coyote or bobcat.

Opposite page:

Unlike its mother, the pronghorn kid has a dappled gray coat.

Joining the Band

Baby pronghorns remain cached for about three weeks. However, if it is safe, they may start coming out after about a week to join in the activities of their mother's group, or band. Usually this band is made up of one buck, several does and several kids.

When the young kids join the band they start playing with the other kids. What a good time they have, running and jumping and butting heads. But all this activity is more than just fun for a pronghorn kid. By running, jumping and chasing it builds up muscles and endurance. The more it plays the stronger and more agile it becomes.

A mother pronghorn enjoys romping with her kids, but she always stays on the alert for any signs of danger.

Babysitting Services

Sometimes the pronghorn mothers want to get away from all this activity for a while. They leave one doe in charge while the rest go off to feed or rest. This pronghorn babysitting system works quite well. Often one doe will be left to watch 10 or 12 kids at a time. When the mothers return, the kids run to them, eager for a drink of warm milk.

Pronghorn kids do not live on just milk for long. Between the ages of three to six weeks, they begin to eat tender green leaves and shoots.

People sometimes mistakenly call pronghorn babies fawns, but this is one kid that is really a kid.

Sun and Scent Signals

Danger! When a pronghorn senses a predator nearby, it often snorts a warning to other pronghorns. It also sends out "sun signals."

To do this, the pronghorn lifts the long hairs of the large white patch on its rump. This raised white patch flashes in the sunshine, warning others who then send out sun signals too. Since pronghorns can see a long way across the prairie, all the pronghorns in the area soon know about the danger.

Pronghorns that are nearby gather in a group and flee from the danger. Usually a doe leads the string of fleeing pronghorns. A large buck runs at the end of the string. He acts as a sort of rear guard. If a coyote or other predator comes near him, he strikes at it with his sharp hoofs or butts it with his horns.

Pronghorns also use scent signals to warn each other of danger. A pronghorn has several scent glands on its body. It can use these to send out scents, or smells, as messages to others.

Growing Up Fast

Baby pronghorns grow up quite quickly. By the age of four months they begin to send sun and scent signals. By fall, when they are about five or six months old, they have stopped nursing and are eating only plants—just like their parents.

The young pronghorns stay with the adult herd for the winter. Together they have a better chance of surviving the howling prairie blizzards and long, cold nights.

When spring arrives, bringing sunshine and new, tender green shoots, the young pronghorns are a year old. By fall they will be old enough to mate. If they are lucky, they will live to enjoy the freedom of their home on the range for three or four more years.

Special Words

Antlers   Solid bony growths that are usually branched.

Buck   Male pronghorn.

Cache   Hiding spot for a newborn pronghorn.

Camouflage   Coloring that blends in with an animal's surroundings so that it can avoid being seen.

Cud   Hastily swallowed food brought back for chewing by cud chewers such as cows, deer and pronghorns.

Doe   Female pronghorn.

Guard hairs   Long coarse hairs that make up the outer layer of the pronghorn's coat.

Hoofs   Feet of pronghorns, deer, cattle and some other animals.

Horns   Outgrowth on a pronghorn's head consisting of hard hollow covers over bony cores.

Kid   Young pronghorn.

Lungs   The part of the body that takes in air and makes it available to the rest of the body.

Mate   To come together to produce young.

Nurse   To drink milk from a mother's body.

Predator   Animal that hunts other animals for food.

INDEX

antelope, 5, 9
baby, *See* kid
babysitting, 43
band, 40
buck, 16, 23, 32, 40, 44

cache, 39, 40
camouflage, 19
coat, 19, 20
color, 19, 44
cud, 28

danger, 44
diet, 28, 43, 46
distribution, 5, 10
doe, 16, 23, 32, 35, 36, 39, 40, 44

endurance, 16
enemies, 19, 24, 36, 44
eyes, 24, 36

fall, 20, 23, 46
female, *See* doe
fighting, 39

group, *See* band
growing up, 46
guard hairs, 20

habitat, 5, 10
heart, 15
hiding place, *See* cache
hoofs, 9, 39, 44
horns, 23, 44

jumping, 31

keeping cool, 20
keeping warm, 20
kid, 6, 35, 36, 40, 43

legend, 5
legs, 15, 36
lifespan, 46
lungs, 15

male, *See* buck
mating, 32, 46
muscles, 15, 16, 20, 40

nursery, 35

playing, 16, 40

range, 5, 46
relatives, 9
running, 6, 12, 15

scent, 36, 39, 44, 46
size, 15
    of newborn, 36
snow, 31
speed, 12
spring, 28, 35, 46
summer, 28, 32
sun signals, 44, 46

territory, 31

weight, 15
winter, 20, 28, 31, 46

Cover Photo: Esther Schmidt (Valan Photos)
Photo Credits: Wilf Schurig (Valan Photos), pages 4, 22; Stephen J. Krasemann
(Valan Photos), pages 7, 42; Wayne Lankinen (Valan Photos), pages 8, 11;
Dennis Schmidt (Valan Photos), pages 13, 14, 18, 25, 30, 45; Tim Fitzharris
(First Light Associated Photographers), pages 17, 21; Esther Schmidt (Valan
Photos), page 26, 33, 34, 38, 41; Don McPhee (Valan Photos), page 29; C. G.
Hampson (Miller Services), page 37.

Getting To Know...

Nature's Children

SEALS

Merebeth Switzer

PUBLISHER	Joseph R. DeVarennes
PUBLICATION DIRECTOR	Kenneth H. Pearson
MANAGING EDITOR	Valerie Wyatt
SERIES ADVISOR	Merebeth Switzer
SERIES CONSULTANT	Michael Singleton
CONSULTANTS	Ross James
	Kay McKeever
	Dr. Audrey N. Tomera
ADVISORS	Roger Aubin
	Robert Furlonger
	Gaston Lavoie
EDITORIAL SUPERVISOR	Jocelyn Smyth
PRODUCTION MANAGER	Ernest Homewood
PRODUCTION ASSISTANTS	Penelope Moir
	Brock Piper

EDITORS

Katherine Farris   Anne Minguet-Patocka
Sandra Gulland   Sarah Reid
Cristel Kleitsch   Cathy Ripley
Elizabeth MacLeod   Eleanor Tourtel
Pamela Martin   Karin Velcheff

PHOTO EDITORS	Bill Ivy
	Don Markle
DESIGN	Annette Tatchell
CARTOGRAPHER	Jane Davie
PUBLICATION ADMINISTRATION	Kathy Kishimoto
	Monique Lemonnier

ARTISTS

Marianne Collins   Greg Ruhl
Pat Ivy   Mary Theberge

This series is approved and recommended by the Federation of Ontario Naturalists.

Canadian Cataloguing in Publication Data

Switzer, Merebeth.
  Seals

(Getting to know—nature's children)
Includes index.
ISBN 0-7172-1910-0

1. Seals (Animals)—Juvenile literature.
I. Title.   II. Series.

QL737.P64S97 1985   j599.74'8   C85-098736-9

Have you ever wondered . . .

how many kinds of seals there are?   page 9

how to tell a seal from a Sea Lion?   page 10

if a seal's hind legs are much use on land?   page 10

where seals are found in North America?   page 13

if seals can move into fresh water?   page 13

how long seals can stay underwater?   page 14

if a seal can dive very deep?   page 17

how seals can keep their eyes open underwater?   page 18

how big seals can be?   page 21

what keeps a seal warm in icy water?   page 22

how seals can manage to go weeks without eating?   page 22

how an overheated seal cools off?   page 24

if there is any way to tell a seal's age?   page 25

if seals have many enemies?   page 25

how mother seals recognize their babies?   page 27

how a seal might say "Who are you?"   page 27

if seals live alone or in groups?   page 28

what a seal's favorite food is?   page 31

what a bearded seal uses its whiskers for?   page 31

if any seals migrate?   page 32

if seal fathers help care for their babies?   page 36

if all baby seals look the same?   page 36

how long most seal mothers look after their babies?   page 42

how male seals attract a mate?   page 45

What barks like a dog, has whiskers like a cat and swims like a fish? If you guessed a seal, congratulations! Seals have an unusual combination of features that equip them for life on land as well as in the water. They are one of the few animals that are at home in both worlds.

When people think about seals they often picture performing seals. But most of the animals that perform in zoos and marine parks are not seals, they are Sea Lions.

The seal, nonetheless, is a superb swimmer. It can do a flashy combination of spins, twirls and somersaults then disappear below the surface in an amazing speed dive.

On land, seals are not as graceful as they are in water. But they seem to enjoy sunbathing and talking to friends, much like vacationers at a beach.

Harbor Seals, like all of us, enjoy relaxing on sandy beaches.

Inquisitive Pups

The sleek, smooth body of the pudgy young seal skims through the water of the harbor. Suddenly it stops and pops its head up to check its surroundings. Its large brown eyes focus on a sailboat gliding quietly by. Overcome by curiosity it watches, bobbing closer to this strange object. Suddenly a flapping sail unfurls. The pup dives deep into the water. Even though it is curious, it will leave this giant sea monster alone!

The young seal's natural curiosity disappears as it grows up and becomes more cautious about the world around it. This is important. In order to survive the pup must learn to be wary.

Is the coast clear? (Gray Seal pup)

Fin-Footed Families

There are many different kinds of seals. They all belong to a group of animals called pinnipeds, which means "fin-footed." You have only to look at their large, flipper-like feet to know why scientists have given them this name. Flippers are much more useful than ordinary feet when you spend as much time in the water as pinnipeds do.

Eared seal

The pinniped group is made up of three families—walruses, eared seals (which include Sea Lions and fur seals) and earless seals, often called true seals. The earless seal family is the biggest and most widespread of the three pinniped families. There are 18 kinds of earless seals and about half of them are found in North America.

Earless seal

Only the Fur Seal has the soft, thick underfur which many people associate with seals, but it is not actually a true or earless seal. Like Sea Lions, it belongs to the eared seal family.

Seal front flipper

Sea Lion front flipper

Opposite page:

When a seal dives, flaps close over its ear openings. (Harbor Seal)

Seal or Sea Lion?

It is not surprising that people sometimes get Seals and Sea Lions confused. But if you look closely, you will spot some differences.

First look at their ears. Sea Lions have ears that are easy to see. No wonder they belong to the group called "eared" seals. Although seals have ears too, their ears are only tiny openings on the sides of their heads. They do not have ear flaps as Sea Lions do.

All Seals and Sea Lions are beautifully streamlined for life in the water, but their hind legs are quite different. As a result, they swim and move on the land in different ways. Sea Lions can walk and even run on land because they can stand on their hind feet. In the water they "row" with their large front flippers and steer with their back feet. Seals use their hind legs as a huge fin to do most of the swimming work.

On land, a seal's hind legs are of little use. Instead of walking, it wriggles along like an overgrown caterpillar.

Creature of Two Worlds

The seal is a creature of two worlds—water and land. It moves with grace and ease through water as it searches for food. Unlike most aquatic animals, it can move from salt water to fresh water if the need arises.

But the seal is a mammal. It needs to breathe air and it must come ashore to mate, to bear its young and to rest.

From the ice floes of the Arctic to the rocky shores of Newfoundland and the sandy beaches of California, the seal lives in areas where water meets land or solid ice.

In North America, seals may be found as far south as New York on the Atlantic Coast and all the way down to California and Mexico on the Pacific Coast.

This Harp Seal pup is quite at home in its frozen world of ice and snow.

Watery Wonder

A seal is wonderfully suited to its watery existence. Its sleek, torpedo-shaped body glides easily through the water and helps make it a first class swimmer.

Seals are remarkable in their ability to remain underwater for long periods of time. Many can stay underwater for about 20 minutes. How do they manage?

Before a seal dives, it breathes out all the air in its body. With no air in its lungs, diving is easier and safer. But the seal's heart and brain, like yours, need oxygen. And like you, the seal can only get oxygen from air. Unlike you, however, the seal can make especially efficient use of the oxygen dissolved in its blood when it is underwater. Until it comes to the surface again to breathe, most of this oxygen goes to its most important body parts—the heart and brain.

World class swimmer. (Harbor Seal)

Diving Champs

Scuba divers must envy seals. Without special equipment, human divers can only go to a depth of 45 metres (150 feet). Diving any deeper is dangerous. But many seals can dive twice as deep as a human. And some, such as the Elephant Seal, can reach depths of about 300 metres (1000 feet).

Your heart beats about 72 times a minute. A seal's heart normally beats much faster, about 150 times per minute. But when the seal dives, its heart rate drops to 60 beats per minute. On very deep or long dives, it may drop as low as 10 to 20 beats per minute. By slowing its heart down in this way, the seal can make its oxygen supply last longer.

Taking a breather. (Harbor Seal)

Beautiful, Beautiful Brown Eyes

The seal's large brown eyes have special features to help it to see underwater. Because it can be very dark deep down in the ocean, the pupils of the seal's eyes open extra wide to let in more light. Out of the water, in bright sunlight, the pupils shrink to a tiny slit.

If you have ever swum in the ocean, you probably know that if you try to keep your eyes open, the salt water will make them sting after a while. Seals do not have this problem. They have an extra, transparent eyelid that they can pull over their eyes to protect them when they are underwater.

Finally, seals do a lot of crying—but not because they are sad. The seal cannot control the tears that flow from its eyes. Just as your eyes water to wash away a speck of dust, the seal's tears flow freely to wash away anything that might irritate its eyes.

Harp Seal

Sizing up Seals

Most types of seals range between one and two metres (3-6 feet) in length and weigh 90 to 225 kilograms (200 to 500 pounds). But male Northern Elephant Seals can grow to more than 6 metres (20 feet) long and weigh as much as 3600 kilograms (8000 pounds). That's longer than most people's living rooms and heavier than two cars! In fact, the Elephant Seal is one of the largest animals in the world.

As is the case with many animals, the males, or bulls, are often much bigger than the females, or cows.

It's no mystery how the large
Northern Elephant Seal got its name.

A Blanket of Blubber

Imagine hopping into a bathtub full of cold water and blocks of ice. Brrr! You would feel like a human icicle seconds after you plunged in! But not seals. Seals can spend long periods of time swimming in freezing water that is often part ice and part water. They are protected by a thick layer of body fat, called blubber, under their skin. A seal's blubber may be up to 15 centimetres (6 inches) thick. This thick blanket of blubber acts as insulation, keeping the seal's body heat in, and the cold out.

Blubber also helps to smooth out the seal's body shape, making it even more streamlined for swimming. And, because it is light, blubber helps keep the seal afloat, so that it does not have to work as hard when swimming.

Seals find their blubber very useful in another way, too. When necessary, they can go weeks without eating, drawing the energy they need from their blubber.

Opposite page:

"Come on in—the water's fine!" (Gray Seal)

22

Air-Conditioning Flippers

Believe it or not a seal is kept so warm by its layer of blubber that it sometimes gets overheated. Since the seal cannot take off its blubber blanket when it gets hot, it has come up with another way to cool off. It gets rid of extra heat through its flippers.

The seal's flippers are not covered with blubber. Instead they are crisscrossed with blood vessels. When the seal gets too warm, it can pump large amounts of blood through its flippers. There the blood is cooled by the surrounding air or water. The cooled blood returns to the body and soon the seal's temperature has returned to normal.

Tell-Tale Teeth

The teeth and claws of seals are made up of
layers, like tree rings. A new layer is added
every year. By counting the layers, scientists
can tell a seal's age. Some seals live up to 40
or more years in the wild.

The seal has few natural enemies, except the
Polar Bear and Killer Whale. Arctic Foxes and
sharks also prey on seals.

Young seals are particularly vulnerable
especially during their first weeks of life. A
Golden Eagle, walrus or other large predator
considers a baby seal an easy meal.

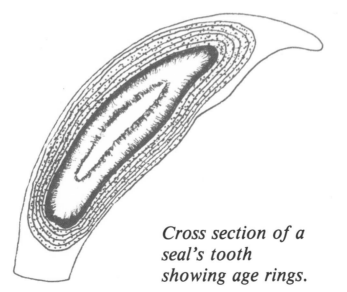

*Cross section of a
seal's tooth
showing age rings.*

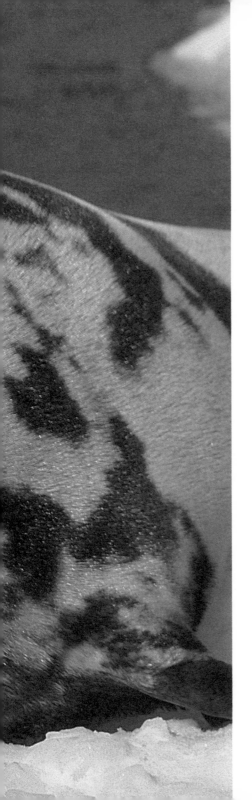

Who Are You?

To us, most seals look a lot alike. It is difficult to tell one from another. Seals seem to have the same problem. On a crowded beach they do not seem to be able to tell their own babies from other babies or friends from strangers just by looking.

Instead, they use smell and sound to help them identify other seals. Most seals have a keen sense of smell. The mother seal uses this to recognize her own baby. This is very important if she is in a large group with other seals and their young.

Seals also use a wide range of calls to find a friend in a crowd. These "Who are you?" calls vary with the type of seal. Some make funny grunts and squeaks while others make dog-like barks.

Hooded Seal

Seals—Alone and Together

When you think of seals, you may think of large groups of them clustered together on a beach. Or you may think of a few seals playing together.

Many seals do live in groups. Some seals gather when ashore but disperse when they return to the water to feed. Others, such as the Harp Seal, spend all their time in groups. During mating and traveling, Harp Seal herds may number thousands of animals.

But other kinds of seals live alone. The Ringed Seal, in particular, spends nearly all of its time on its own. The mother gives birth to one baby in a secluded den she digs under the snow or in a natural hollow in the ice. Mother and baby stay together for about two months. Except for this time, however, and a brief time spent with a mate, the Ringed Seal remains alone.

Harbor Seals

Seal-Time Meal-Time

Since seals search for food in the water, you can probably guess one of their favorite foods. That's right—fish.

But seals eat other foods as well. Harbor Seals search in tidepools for small sea creatures left behind by the outgoing tide. The ocean-roaming Harp Seal eats small fish such as herring and capelin and masses of tiny, shrimp-like animals called krill.

Many seals prefer to eat bottom-living animals such as crabs, clams, whelks, shrimp, snails and octopuses. In fact, the Bearded Seal has special whiskers like the walrus's to help it search for tasty treats on the dark ocean bottom. Scientists think that it rakes up the bottom with its front claws and then uses its whiskers to sift through the debris. When the Bearded Seal finds a yummy whelk or succulent clam it uses it strong jaws and teeth to crush the shell to get at the food. Since it does not need the shell in its diet, it spits out the broken pieces.

Opposite page:

A seal's whiskers are sensitive feelers that help it find food in the murky ocean depths. (Harbor Seal)

31

Long Journeys

You probably know that many birds migrate, traveling south at about the same time every fall, then north again in the spring. But did you know that some seals do the same thing? When winter comes, seals that live in large groups in Arctic waters must migrate to find food. Some of them may travel hundreds of kilometres.

The Harp Seal is probably the best known migrator. In summer, when northern waters teem with small fish and tiny marine animals, Harp Seals live and feed in the water at the edge of the Arctic pack ice. In fall, as the ice begins to spread southward over their feeding grounds, the seals move southward ahead of it. Then in spring they follow the melting edge northward again.

Not all kinds of seals migrate. Those that live alone or in small groups have little need to make these long seasonal journeys in search of food.

Harp Seal and pup.

Birth Time

Baby seals may be born at different times of year, depending on the type of seal and where its home is. Most seal mothers, however, give birth in late winter. They haul themselves out onto the ice or onto land to have their babies.

Some cows gather in large groups to have their babies, others give birth alone. In either case, the bulls usually stay away from the females at this time. They may form bachelor groups or go off by themselves. They do not help care for the babies when they are born.

With a pup this young, mom is probably not far away.(Harbor Seal)

Meet the Baby

The seal babies, or pups, are quite small compared to their mothers. Ringed Seal babies may weigh as little as four and a half kilograms (10 pounds), while Bearded Seal pups may weigh as much as 36 kilograms (80 pounds).

Most seals that are born on ice or snow have a soft woolly white coat. This is very important for it will keep them warm until their bodies have a chance to build up a layer of blubber. A white coat also helps the pup blend into its snowy home, so that it is not easily spotted by predators.

Seals that are born on cliffs or sandy beaches are usually a dark brown or mottled color. This helps them blend in with the rocky or sandy beaches on which they spend the first weeks of their life.

A Harbor Seal's pup is usually born with a coat very much like that of its mother.

A Caring Mother

Baby seals begin to feed on their mother's milk minutes after they are born. Some nurse in the water, others on land or on ice floes. The milk is so rich that it looks just like soft creamy butter.

Most baby seals do not spend a long time with their mother, but while they do, they are well cared for. The mother stays near her baby, ready for its almost constant demands to nurse. If she does leave for any reason, she is seldom gone for long.

Getting to know each other.
(Harbor Seal mother and pup)

38

Swimming Lessons

Seals are natural swimmers, but this does not mean that they jump right into the water. This strange new wetness requires a close checking before the first plunge. The curious pup sidles up to the water's edge and after a sniff and sidelong glance it dumps its body in. The flustered baby bobs in the water unsure of its new surroundings. Soon, though, it will be swimming with the same ease and grace as its parents. When it needs a rest a tired pup may hitch a ride on its mother's shoulders.

Hooded Seal pups are called bluebacks because of their blue-tinged fur.

A Hasty Departure

Some pups have two months or more of their mother's care, but many are left to fend for themselves when they are about two weeks old. These pups are well prepared for life on their own, however. They are already at home in the water, and most have grown-up teeth for feeding. In other words, they have all the tools they need to survive. They simply need to learn how to use them. And until they do learn to catch their own food, they can live off their blubber.

There are reasons for the mother seal's rather hasty departure. If she is to have another baby next year, she has to seek out a male to mate with. Also, the cow seal has not eaten since giving birth. In supplying milk for her baby, she has already used up a great deal of her body fat. If she is to survive to mate, she must stop nursing her young.

Opposite page:

When a male Hooded Seal inflates the elastic skin over its nose into a "hood", it is warning intruders to stay away.

Mating Time

Mating usually takes place a few weeks after the cows have left their pups. At this time the cows and bulls seek each other out. Some bulls will put on spectacular swimming displays to impress a female, and often two bulls will fight each other to determine who will father the young.

Among some types of seals, a powerful bull may set up a harem of several cows. He will mate with the cows in his harem and protect them from the advances of other males. At first he will probably just try to discourage an intruding male by lowering his head and hissing. If that does not work, he will fight. Usually the intruder gives up before anyone is seriously hurt.

During the mating season some male seals give off a powerful musky odor. As unappealing as this smells to us, it works to attract female seals.

Opposite page:

Within two to three weeks after birth the long cream-colored coat of this Gray Seal pup will be shed, and replaced with a much darker coat similar to that of its parents.

New Coats for Old

After the adult seals mate, they shed their coats. By this time their old coats are ragged and shaggy. They have been worn away in many places over the past year. In some cases the coat sheds in large pieces, sometimes taking old, dead outer skin with it.

While they are molting, the seals rest and remain on land. They do not eat. Instead, they live off their stores of blubber. Within a few weeks, the bulls and cows have grown new coats of coarse fur.

It is now time to return to the ocean for their first meal in a long time. The seals head out in search of food. Most will live out in the ocean until next spring when they will again haul themselves out onto the land or ice where the next generation of pups will be born.

Special Words

Bull   Male seal.

Cow   Female seal.

Ice Floes   Large floating pieces of flat ice.

Lungs   The part of the body that takes oxygen from the air and makes it available to the rest of the body.

Mating   Coming together to produce young.

Migration   Traveling at regular times of the year in search of food or a place to give birth.

Molt   To shed a coat of fur and grow another.

Nurse   To drink milk from a mother's body.

Oxygen   The part of the air that is used by the body.

Pinnipeds   A group of animals whose legs are specially shaped as flippers. Seals, Sea Lions and walruses are pinnipeds.

Predator   Animal that hunts other animals for food.

Pup   Young seal.

Pupil   The inner circle of the eye, which opens and closes to take in light.

Tidepool   A pool of water left on the shore when the tide goes out.

INDEX

appearance, 5, 10

Bearded Seal, 31, 36
blubber, 22, 24, 42
breathing, 13, 14
bull, 21, 35, 45

California Fur Seal, *illus.* 8
calls, 27
claws, 25, 31
coats, 36, 46
cooling off, 24
cow, 21, 27, 28, 35, 38, 41, 42, 45
curiosity, 6, 41

den, 28
diet, 22, 31, 42, 46
distribution, 9, 13; *map*, 13
diving, 17

eared seals, 9, 10
ears, 10; *illus.* 10
Elephant Seal, 17, 21; *illus.* 20
enemies, 25
eyes, 18

fighting, 45
flippers, 9, 10, 22; *illus.* 10

Gray Seal, *illus.* 7, 23, 44
groups, 28, 32
growing up, 38, 42

habitat, 13, 46
Harbor Seal, 31
   illus. 4, 11, 15, 16, 30, 34, 39
harem, 45
Harp Seal, 28, 31, 32; *illus.* 12, 19, 33
heart rate, 17
Hooded Seal, *illus.* 40, 43

insulation, 22

mating, 28, 42
migration, 32
molting, 46
musk, 45

pup, 6, 25, 27, 28, 35, 36, 38, 41, 42

relatives, 9
Ringed Seal, 8, 36

Sea Lions, 5, 9, 10
senses, 27
shape, 14, 22
size, 21, 36
spring, 46
staying underwater, 14
swimming, 5, 10, 14, 22, 41, 45

teeth, 25, 31, 41; *illus.* 25

walruses, 9, 31
whiskers, 31
winter, 32, 35

Cover Photo: Kennon Cooke

Photo Credits: Harold V. Green (Valan Photos), page 4; Val and Alan Wilkinson (Valan Photos), pages 7, 34; Stephen J. Krasemann (Valan Photos), pages 8, 37; Kennon Cooke (Valan Photos), page 11; Fred Bruemmer, pages 12, 20, 23, 33, 39, 43; Michel Bourque (Valan Photos), page 15; François Lepine (Valan Photos), page 16; Norman Lightfoot (Eco-Art Productions), page 19; W. Hoek (Valan Photos), page 26; Wamboldt-Waterfield (Miller Services), page 29; Esther Schmidt (Valan Photos), page 30; Valan Photos, page 40; Anthony J. Bond (Valan Photos), page 44.